# true love PROJECT

## HOW THE GOSPEL DEFINES YOUR PURITY

CLAYTON & SHARIE KING

ISBN: 978-1-4158-7828-6
Item: 005558778

Dewey Decimal Classification Number: 306.73
Subject Headings: CHRISTIAN LIFE \ SEXUAL ABSTINENCE \ GOSPEL


Printed in the United States of America



Student Ministry Publishing
LifeWay Church Resources
One LifeWay Plaza
Nashville, TN 37234-0144

We believe that the Bible has God for its author; salvation for its end; and truth, without any mixture of error, for its matter
and that all Scripture is totally true and trustworthy.
To review LifeWay's doctrinal guideline, please visit *www.lifeway.com/doctrinalguideline*.


All Scripture quotations are taken from the Holman Christian Standard Bible Copyright 1999, 2000, 2002, 2003, 2009 by
Holman Bible Publishers.
Used by permission.

# table of contents

# about the authors

**CLAYTON KING** is President of Crossroads Ministries, the Teaching Pastor at Newspring Church, and Campus Pastor at Liberty University. He is an evangelist, author, and missionary. Clayton began preaching at the age of 14 and has traveled to 36 countries and 46 states. He's written nine books and preached to over three million people. Clayton is passionate about seeing people far from God repent of their sin and begin a relationship with Jesus. He loves to pastor pastors and empower Christians for ministry. He also loves four-wheelers, action figures, black coffee, and his wife and two sons. For more information about Clayton and his ministries, visit him at claytonking.com and crossroadsworldwide.com

**SHARIE KING** was saved at the age of 11 and sensed God calling her to share her story of rescue and redemption. She has shared the gospel at Crossroads camps, college campuses, and mission trips in countries like Poland, India, and Malaysia. Sharie speaks at women's events in local churches and conferences across America, teaching on marriage and ministry with her husband, Clayton. She also speaks on sexual purity, finding your identity in Christ, and overcoming fear. Sharie has a heart to see women embrace the truth of the gospel. She loves painting, writing, and homeschooling her two boys. For more about Sharie, visit her at sharieking.com

# note from the authors

Students today may not be aware that the Bible holds to the belief that sex is an intrinsically good thing. In fact, they also may not be aware that God gave it to them as a gift to be shared in the proper context of marriage. Students rarely hear that sex and purity actually reflect the glory of God, and our beliefs about these things influence our witness to those around us.

The task of living for the glory of God is a tremendous challenge for any Christian, at any age. It's even more difficult in a culture that constantly markets lust, sex, and pornography. In light of competing voices and easy access to commit sexual sin, trying to avoid sexual temptation can seem nearly impossible.

The truth is, it is impossible...if one tries to do it on his or her own. It is impossible... if one doesn't understand why he or she should live according to God's story. It is impossible...if one doesn't know how to fight against sexual sins. It is impossible...if one doesn't understand how to fight for holiness and purity. It is impossible...if one doesn't know who he or she is and Who he or she belongs to.

However, these things are not impossible when we understand who God is and who He made us to be. If we belong to Jesus Christ and His Spirit is in us, that means that He is with us and He is for you. God has a greater purpose for our lives than we could ever imagine. When we see ourselves as created by God, for God, on purpose, and for a purpose, it changes everything. When we see our story in light of God's, we gain a sense of meaning. Our lives matters, and so does what we do with our bodies.

For those students who are beginning to understand and explore their sexuality, this study is for them—to guide them to purity and holiness by submitting their future to the lordship of Christ. If many of them feel dirty and condemned because they didn't wait, this study is also for them—to show them the mercy and grace of Jesus Christ and to help them walk in His forgiveness as a new person.

I pray that you and your students will benefit from these pages, that you both will find comfort, hope, and peace in submitting to the lordship of Jesus, and that your identity and purity will be anchored in the perfect work of Christ for you on the cross.

# how to use this study

Welcome to the *True Love Project*. Over the course of these sessions, you and your students will be exposed to what God has to say about issues pertaining to sex, romance, and purity, while also showing the centrality of Christ in all these things.

Before you begin, it is worth mentioning that the *True Love Project* is a unique resource from among our other short-term studies. The biggest difference has to do with the way the sessions are laid out. It is designed for your students to have a deeper level of interaction with the material, as well as a more meaningful time for group discussion. For a detailed outline for how each session progresses, see Session Elements and Sequence below.

++Whenever this background appears, this indicates that the content is also in the student book.

## WHAT YOU'LL NEED:

+ DVD player / TV or data projector
+ *True Love Project* DVD (Leader Kit)
+ *True Love Project* Student Book and pen for each student
+ *True Love Project* Leader Guides

## INTRO SESSION

This session is used to introduce the *True Love Project* to students. The elements and sequence in this session will vary from normal sessions. See the Intro Session page for this session's sequence.

## SESSION ELEMENTS & SEQUENCE (FOR SESSIONS 1 - 8)

## 1) Session Introduction (APPROXIMATELY FIVE MINUTES)
   ◆ Provides an opening discussion starter to begin each session.

## 2) Video Recap (APPROXIMATELY FIVE MINUTES)
   ◆ Provides a transition to the session interview by giving a brief recap of each session's teaching segment, highlighting the teaching points and main thought.

## 3) Session Interview 💿 DVD (APPROXIMATELY 10 MINUTES)
   ◆ Eight interviews are provided featuring Clayton and Sharie King talking with

various church leaders.

- Interviews are informal and conversational, focusing on each respective session theme.
- Space is provided for students to take notes in their student books.

## 4) Group Discussion (APPROXIMATELY 25 MINUTES)

- During Group Discussion you will...
  ...briefly discuss the interview
  ...review the Video Guide and Video Feedback from the teaching session
  ...consider other questions provided to enhance the discussion
  ...lead students to summarize the truths of each lesson and briefly discuss
  ...provide students opportunity to apply what they have learned by
      listing action points
- Feel free to conduct the Group Discussion in a large group setting or in gender-specific small groups.

- There is a Group Discussion Page for each session in the student book to help guide students through this portion of the study.

## 5) Session Teaching 💿 DVD (APPROXIMATELY 15 MINUTES)

- Eight teaching segments with Clayton King, one per session.
- These teaching segments contain the heart of each session, making it a vital part of the *True Love Project* experience.
- **Students will watch the teaching segment the week before the actual session.** At the end of the Intro Session, they will watch Session One teaching. At the end of Session One, they will watch Session Two teaching, and so forth.
- Students are provided a Video Guide for each session in their student book to help record the main points of Clayton's teaching.
- Students are given a Video Feedback and Reflect sections in their student book pertaining to each session. It is encouraged that students complete these sections on their own time.

## STUDENT BOOKS

Each student should have a *True Love Project* student book. The student book provides students:

- space to record key points and feedback from the teaching segments
- a place to take notes on the interviews
- additional material to study on their own (i.e. Video Feedback and Reflect sections)
- a Group Discussion page

# intro session

1) Welcome
2) Intro Video 📀
3) Discussion Starter
4) God's Story, Your Story 📀

## 1) Welcome

This is the first time your group will be together for the *True Love Project*. Since this session serves as the intro and is shorter than the rest of the sessions, you may want to consider planning a cookout or other kind of informal fellowship to begin the study. You will also want to distribute a student book and pen to each student.

## 2) Intro Video 📀

After a time of welcoming, play the Intro Video for your group.

## 3) Discussion Starter

After the Intro Video, break your students into groups divided by gender to discuss the following questions. After allowing some time for students to discuss, bring the groups back and allow them the opportunity to share with everyone.

✝ Why do you think people often say that we live in a very sexualized culture?
✝ Do you feel there is both spoken and unspoken pressure for students to be sexually active? Explain.
✝ How would you define sexual purity? Why is sexual purity more than just remaining a virgin?
✝ How do you view sexual purity in light of your relationship with Christ?

## 4) God's Story, Your Story 📀

After the discussion starter, explain to students that even though this is a study about sex and purity, we would start off on the wrong foot if we began by talking about such things. Think of it this way: you wouldn't start your first day of Biology class with a dissection. Rather, you would begin by getting the bigger picture of the study of Biology. By gaining a bird's-eye view of the subject, you build a foundation that will help you understand dissections down the road.

Similarly, before we jump into the topics of sex and purity, we must first understand God's larger story. It is then that we will have the foundation to understand our own sexuality and purity.

Play the DVD segment "God's Story, Your Story." Guide students to page 6 in their student books to follow along (p. 12 in the leader guide). After the video teaching, encourage students to complete the Video Feedback, as well as the Reflect sections in their books before the next session. Explain that these sections will be used for group discussion at the next meeting. Close with prayer.

**1**

# session 1:
# GOD'S STORY, YOUR STORY

This study isn't primarily about issues related to sex, purity, and romance. Primarily, it is about helping you understand those things in light of God's eternal, bigger story. Only when you are able to see your role in that story will you know what God wants to do with you and through you.

## SESSION 1 SEQUENCE:

1) Session Introduction
2) Video Recap
3) Session Interview 💿 DVD
4) Group Discussion
5) The Cost of Ownership 💿 DVD

## 1) Session Introduction (APPROXIMATELY FIVE MINUTES)

Begin the first session by welcoming students and thanking them for being a part of the *True Love Project*. If there are any new students who have joined since the Intro Session, be sure to provide them with a student book.

Once everyone has settled in, begin a discussion with students based on the following questions:

✝ What are your top five favorite books and/or movies? How did these get to the top of your list? Why do you find them so compelling?

After spending a few minutes discussing these questions, explain to them that often what people find most compelling in a movie or a book is the story that is being told—and the better the story, the more we find ourselves being drawn into it.

## 2) Video Recap (APPROXIMATELY FIVE MINUTES)

To transition to the session interview, remind students that the first teaching segment laid the groundwork for a gospel foundation so that we can begin to think about the issues of sex, romance, and purity in light of God's story. We looked at God's original intention for these issues (creation), what went wrong (the fall), and His plan to make all things new through Christ (redemption and restoration). In the end, this lesson helps us understand how our stories fit into His bigger story, thus giving us purpose, clarity, and direction when it comes to understanding our own sexuality.

## Main Thought:

An understanding of sex and purity begins with an understanding of God's story and your role in it.

## 3) Session Interview 💿 (APPROXIMATELY 10 MINUTES)

After the recap/summary, play the session interview with Mark Batterson. Direct students to the group discussion page in their student books (p. 12). Point out the space provided for notes on the interview. Record some of your personal reflections below to discuss during Group Discussion.

## 4) Group Discussion (APPROXIMATELY 25 MINUTES)

+ Briefly discuss highlights from the interview.

+ Review the Video Guide and Video Feedback from Session 1 in the leader guide (pp. 12-13).

+ Use the following questions to enhance your discussion.

++
Remember, whenever you see content with this background, it indicates it is also located in the student book.

• Why is it important to begin this study by focusing on God rather than on the topic at hand?

• Why do the topics of sex and purity make more sense in the context of God's larger story? Why is it important to know that our lives are part of something much bigger than ourselves?

• What is the difference between the third and fourth act of God's story?

• What does Clayton mean when he talks about understanding your individual story in light of God's bigger story?

• What has God been restoring in your life?

+ Direct students to complete the Highlights section of the Group Discussion page in their student books (p. 12). Allow time to answer and discuss these as a group.

+ **ASK:** What actions do you need to take in response to what you have learned? Encourage students to list their answers under the Action Points. Below is a sample to prompt students.

### Action Points

+ Begin looking at people of the opposite sex as image bearers of God, and not merely as objects of attraction.

+

+

# Session 1: GOD'S STORY, YOUR STORY

This may sound strange, but we are going to begin our study on purity, sex, and romance by not talking about purity, sex, or romance. There's no doubt that the things we talk about in this lesson are directly related to issues of physical intimacy, but in order to correctly tackle the issues surrounding sex and purity, it is essential that we first begin with the One who created these things. By understanding God's story, we will gain a better understanding of ourselves and how our individual stories fit into His larger story.

# video guide:

## CREATION

God made us because He <u>wanted</u> to.

You were fashioned and designed to <u>look</u> like God.

## FALL

We see in Adam and Eve a <u>reflection</u> of our own selves. We think we know better than <u>Him</u>.

We believe He is <u>withholding</u> something from us that would make us happier.

## REDEMPTION

The word that best describes this process of being rescued from sin and destruction is "<u>redemption</u>."

In essence, it refers to the fact that Jesus <u>lived</u> the perfect life we could never <u>live</u>.

## RESTORATION

Part of this restoration means He wants to <u>restore</u> us to the place He originally intended us to be.

Restoration touches every part of your life, repairing your perspective on <u>love</u> and <u>relationships</u>.

# video feedback:

+ Why would it be important to begin a study on purity and sex with a discussion about God's story?

+ What does Clayton mean when he talks about understanding your individual story in light of God's bigger story?

+ How does each of the story elements (creation, fall, redemption, restoration) speak directly to issues of relationships, sexuality, purity, etc.?

**CREATION:**

**FALL:**

**REDEMPTION:**

**RESTORATION:**

+ What do these story elements communicate about God's character and intention for people?

Develop and post a personal tweet or Facebook status related to this session using the hashtag **#trueloveproject**

## 5) The Cost of Ownership  (APPROXIMATELY 15 MINUTES)

Once group discussion has ended, watch the DVD segment *The Cost of Ownership*. Instruct students to turn to page 14 in their student books to follow along. After the session, help students complete their video guides if they missed any points.

After the video, encourage students to complete both the Video Feedback and Reflect sections in Session 2 of the student book before the next time you meet. Explain that these sections will be used in group discussion during the next session. Close your time together in prayer.

## Leader Notes

From Clayton's teaching and your personal reflection, what are some highlights you intend to discuss during group time?

**2**

# THE COST OF OWNERSHIP

in
the
as a
sation
g was

ket to
, and

ould

"Before you can understand love, you must understand lordship. Before you decide who you will love, you must decide who is your Lord."

**-CLAYTON KING**

1) Session Introduction
2) Video Recap
3) Session Interview 💿 DVD
4) Group Discussion
5) The Bible on Sex 💿 DVD

# 1) Session Introduction (APPROXIMATELY FIVE MINUTES)

Begin the session by welcoming students and thanking them for being a part of the *True Love Project*. Once everyone has settled in, begin a discussion with students based on the follow questions:

✛ Who are the authorities in your life? Do you respond well to these authorities? Why or why not?

✛ What does it mean for Jesus to be the Lord of your life? Can He be Lord of just part of your life? Explain.

After spending a few minutes discussing these questions, explain that many of us struggle with authority. We want to be our own bosses. But when it comes to our relationship with Jesus, He must be Lord of every area of our lives. Keep this in mind: If Jesus is not Lord of all, He's not Lord at all.

# 2) Video Recap (APPROXIMATELY FIVE MINUTES)

To transition to the session interview, recap Clayton's teaching session by reminding students that Jesus' lordship relates to our beliefs and actions on the issues of sex, romance, and purity. In addition, remind students of the contrast between having Jesus as Lord and being your own lord, and why it is better to submit to Jesus' lordship as opposed to following the sinful impulses of your own heart.

## Main Thought:

Because Jesus is the main character in God's story, we should follow His lordship and recognize that He knows best when it comes to sex and purity.

## 3) Session Interview 📀 (APPROXIMATELY 10 MINUTES)

After the recap/summary, play the session interview with Perry Noble. Direct students to the group discussion page in their student books (p. 20). Point out the space provided for notes on the interview. Record some of your personal reflections below to discuss during Group Discussion.

## 4) Group Discussion (APPROXIMATELY 25 MINUTES)

✝ Briefly discuss highlights from the interview.

✝ Review the Video Guide and Video Feedback from Session 2 in the leader guide (pp. 18-19).

✝ Use the following questions to enhance your discussion.

> • What is something you have learned about yourself during this session?
>
> • How would you respond to someone who said that it is possible to have Jesus as Savior but not as Lord?
>
> • Why does the issue of lordship affect so many aspects of your life? What does life look like if you are lord? What does life look like if Jesus is Lord?

✝ Direct students to complete the Highlights section of the Group Discussion page in their student books (p. 20). Allow time to answer and discuss these as a group.

✝ **ASK:** What actions do you need to take in response to what you've learned? Encourage students to list answers under Action Points. Below is a sample to prompt students.

### Action Points

✝ Live life in such a way that shows Jesus is seen as being first and foremost in my relationships.

✝

✝

## Session 2: THE COST OF OWNERSHIP

As we learned in the first session, we are all part of God's redemptive story. We are being remade as we experience redemption through His Son. In this session, we will discover that the main character in God's story is His Son, Jesus. Because of who Jesus is, we should submit to His lordship over our lives and recognize that He knows best when it comes to issues of sex and purity.

# video guide:

Every single important thing in your life revolves around one issue, and that is the issue of lordship.

Whoever has the title of Lord in your life is the ultimate ruler and calls all the shots.

## FOLLOW HIS LORDSHIP:

When Jesus is Lord, you recognize the sacrifice He made when He died in your place to reconcile you to God.

When Jesus is Lord, you want to honor His Word in your relationships and live by His rules that govern your body and sexual desires.

When you are Lord, you're driven primarily by whatever it is that you want at any given moment.

If you are the lord of your life, then you are the ultimate authority and you become a god unto yourself.

## RECOGNIZE THAT HE KNOWS BEST WHEN IT COMES TO SEX AND PURITY:

Because He cares about you and because He knows best (and can see the consequences of your sins and bad decisions), He invites you to give control of your life to Him.

Before you can understand love, you must understand lordship.

Before you decide who you will love, you must decide who is your Lord.

# video feedback:

✛ Summarize what it means for Jesus to be Lord over your life. What are the implications in the areas of romance and intimacy?

✛ What signs might indicate that you are lord over your life? What signs might indicate that Jesus is Lord over your life?

✛ Why is trying to be lord over your life detrimental to your health? Why is it actually good and joyful to have Jesus be your Lord?

✛ How was C.S. Lewis' story about children playing near the edge of the cliff helpful in thinking about how God relates to His children? Do you believe that God is working for your good and joy? Why or why not?

Develop and post a personal tweet or Facebook status related to this session using the hashtag **#trueloveproject**

## 5) The Bible on Sex  (APPROXIMATELY 15 MINUTES)

Once group discussion has ended, watch the DVD segment *The Bible on Sex*. Instruct students to turn to page 22 in their student books to follow along. After the session, help students complete their video guides if they missed any points.

After the video, encourage students to complete both the Video Feedback and Reflect sections in Session 3 of the student book before the next time you meet. Explain that these sections will be used in group discussion during the next session. Close your time together in prayer.

## Leader Notes

From Clayton's teaching and your personal reflection, what are some highlights you intend to discuss during group time?

# 3

in
the
as a
sation
g was

ket to
e, and

would

# session 3:
# THE BIBLE
# ON SEX

Then the LORD God said "It is not good for the man
to be alone. I will make a helper as his complement."

**GENESIS 2:18**

## SESSION 3 SEQUENCE

1) Session Introduction
2) Video Recap
3) Session Interview 💿 DVD
4) Group Discussion
5) Your Heart Matters 💿 DVD

## 1) Session Introduction (APPROXIMATELY FIVE MINUTES)

Welcome students to the session and begin by discussing the following questions:

✛ What are the top songs on the radio right now? What are the top movies that are currently playing? What are some of your favorite TV shows?

✛ Considering these forms of media, what are some of the messages they are sending concerning sexuality?

Discuss how we don't have to listen long or look far to clearly see the huge difference that exists between how our culture views sexuality versus how the Bible sees it.

## 2) Video Recap (APPROXIMATELY FIVE MINUTES)

To transition to the session interview, recap Clayton's teaching regarding the contrast between the cultural and biblical views of sex and purity. Remind students that there are a lot of cultural misconceptions surrounding sex, the two most predominant views being that sex is everything or sex is nothing. However, when it comes to submitting to the lordship of Jesus, we are also submitting to what Scripture says about these topics. The Bible declares that sex is a good gift to be enjoyed between a man and a woman in the lifelong covenant of marriage.

### Main Thought:

While culture teaches that sex is either everything or nothing, the Bible teaches that sex is good and a gift.

## 3) Session Interview 📀 (APPROXIMATELY 10 MINUTES)

After the recap/summary, play the session interview with Jud and Lori Wilhite. Direct students to the group discussion page in their student books (p. 28). Point out the space provided for notes on the interview. Record some of your personal reflections below to discuss during Group Discussion.

## 4) Group Discussion (APPROXIMATELY 25 MINUTES)

✛ Briefly discuss highlights from the interview

✛ Review the Video Guide and Video Feedback from Session 3 in the leader guide (pp. 24-25).

✛ Use the following questions to enhance your discussion.

- How does culture influence our beliefs regarding sex and purity? How do our past experiences influence those beliefs?

- How is the Bible's view of sex within marriage better than culture's view?

- What did you learn about the Bible's perspective on sex and purity from this session? How did it challenge you?

- Why is it important to learn about sex from the One who designed it? What advantages does this bring?

✛ Direct students to complete the Highlights section of the Group Discussion page in their student books (p. 28). Allow time to answer and discuss these as a group.

✛ **ASK:** What actions do you need to take in response to what you've learned? Encourage students to list answers under Action Points. Below is a sample to prompt students.

### Action Points

✛ Filter any messages regarding sex and romance from culture and/or peers through the grid of God's Word.

✛

✛

# Session 3: THE BIBLE ON SEX

It comes as no surprise that our culture sends a confusing message regarding sex, romance, and intimacy. Instead of supporting the biblical view that sex is good and is a gift, it promotes the misunderstanding that sex is everything or is nothing at all. However, if we, under the lordship of Christ, are to understand our sexuality in light of God's original design and intention, then we must turn to what the Bible has to say on the subject.

## video guide:

### SEX IS NOT EVERYTHING:

When sex is everything, the result is sexual obsession.

### SEX IS NOT NOTHING:

This perspective places sex in a category of shameful and nasty things that make you feel yucky.

For some, sex is completely empty, and the result is sexual confusion.

### SEX IS A GIFT:

Sex is a good gift that is given to us by a good God who intentionally created sex as a means of pleasure and procreation.

Sexual intimacy was engineered in the mind of God as a gift to His children.

### SEX IS GOOD:

It came from God, and God gives good things to His children.

God instigated sex in the institution of marriage, even commanding Adam and Eve to come together physically.

For us, sex is a good gift that is waiting for us in the relationship of marriage.

# video feedback:

+ What are some misconceptions regarding sex in culture today?


+ Why do you think the biblical portrait of sex is often overlooked and set aside within our culture?


+ Why would it be unfulfilling to view sex as "everything"?


+ Why would it be unfulfilling to view sex as "nothing"?


+ Why is it important to emphasize that God is the Author of sex and that He created it as a good gift?


+ How can the biblical portrait of sex (as good and as a gift) lead to a life that is both fulfilling and honoring to Christ?


Develop and post a personal tweet or Facebook status related to this session using the hashtag #trueloveproj

# 5) Your Heart Matters  (APPROXIMATELY 15 MINUTES)

Once group discussion has ended, watch the DVD segment *Your Heart Matters*. Instruct students to turn to page 30 in their student books to follow along. After the session, help students complete their video guides if they missed any points.

After the video, encourage students to complete both the Video Feedback and Reflect sections in Session 4 of the student book before the next time you meet. Explain that these sections will be used in group discussion during the next session. Close your time together in prayer.

# Leader Notes

From Clayton's teaching and your personal reflection, what are some highlights you intend to discuss during group time?

**4**

in
the
as a
sation
g was

ket to
, and

vould

# session 4:
# YOUR HEART
# MATTERS

For from within, out of people's hearts, come
evil thoughts, sexual immoralities, thefts, murders,
adulteries, greed, evil actions, deceit, promiscuity,
stinginess, blasphemy, pride, and foolishness. All these
evil things come from within and defile a person.

**MARK 7:21-23**

1) Session Introduction
2) Video Recap
3) Session Interview 💿 DVD
4) Group Discussion
5) Purity From Within 💿 DVD

# 1) Session Introduction (APPROXIMATELY FIVE MINUTES)

Begin Session 4 by grouping students into small teams. Distribute a sheet of paper to each team and share the following assignment:

✛ For the next three minutes, work as a team to list as many phrases, sayings, or song lyrics that you can think of that contain the word *heart*. For instance, "I love you with all my heart," or "You gotta have heart."

After three minutes, allow teams to share their lists. Guide students to mark out the items on their lists that are shared by other teams. Give a prize to the team with the most unique listings. Discuss how easy it is to see that the heart plays a big role in our lives, relationships, and the decisions we make.

# 2) Video Recap (APPROXIMATELY FIVE MINUTES)

To transition to the session interview, recap Clayton's teaching session by reminding students about what the Bible says regarding the human heart, particularly when it comes to issues of sex and purity. In essence, all sinful actions are an overflow of the heart, and in order to experience change in behavior, a genuine heart change is first needed. Finally, remind students that the reason this is so important is because it shows us how we should respond to sexual sin within our lives. In other words, if we only try to correct the behavior, we will never succeed since the problem lies within the heart.

## Main Thought:

When it comes to the human heart, the Bible teaches us that it is the command center of one's life, deceitful and corrupt, and made new in Christ.

# 3) Session Interview 📀 (APPROXIMATELY 10 MINUTES)

After the recap/summary, play the session interview with Ocielia Gibson. Direct students to the group discussion page in their student books (p. 36). Point out the space provided for notes on the interview. Record some of your personal reflections below to discuss during Group Discussion.

# 4) Group Discussion (APPROXIMATELY 25 MINUTES)

✛ Briefly discuss highlights from the interview.

✛ Review the Video Guide and Video Feedback from Session 4 in the leader guide (pp. 30-31).

✛ Use the following questions to enhance your discussion.

- What have you learned about your own heart from this session?

- Why is it not enough to focus merely on a change of behavior when dealing with sexual sins? Why must we also focus on a change of heart?

- Do you consider it good news or bad news that you alone can't change your heart, but that the grace of God is needed? Explain.

- Have you allowed God to change your heart? Why or why not?

✛ Direct students to complete the Highlights section of the Group Discussion page in their student books (p. 36). Allow time to answer and discuss these as a group.

✛ **ASK:** What actions do you need to take in response to what you've learned? Encourage students to list answers under Action Points. Below is a sample to prompt students.

## Action Points

✛ Quit pursuing change through personal strength alone. Realize it comes from God and pursue it through Christ.

✛

✛

# Session 4: YOUR HEART MATTERS

Often absent from discussions about sex and purity are in-depth conversations about why we do the things we do. In other words, when it comes to making decisions about what we do with our bodies, it is important that we understand the role of our hearts in the decision-making process. By understanding the corruption of our hearts, we will be in a better position to see how our hearts function as the command center of our lives. We will also realize our desperate need to have our hearts made new in Christ.

## video guide:

### COMMAND CENTER OF YOUR LIFE:

When it comes to the biblical understanding of the heart, we need to realize that the heart is more than just the center of our human <u>affections</u>.

The heart is the <u>command</u> center of human life. It controls and influences <u>everything</u> a person does.

### DECEITFUL AND CORRUPT:

When we think about our hearts, we assume that they are <u>innocent</u> and filled with <u>love</u>.

"The heart is more <u>deceitful</u> than anything else, and incurable—who can understand it?" Jeremiah 17:9

You need to realize that you really don't have a <u>lust</u> problem, a sex problem, a pornographic problem, or a <u>behavioral</u> problem. What you really have is a <u>heart</u> problem.

### MADE NEW IN CHRIST:

The good news is that the power of the <u>gospel</u> can change our sick, deceitful hearts and make them brand new.

<u>Jesus</u> is the cure for your heart problem.

# video feedback:

+ Have you ever thought about the central role your heart plays in forming your beliefs about sex and purity? Why or why not?

+ Why would it be important to talk about the role of the heart in making decisions regarding sexual purity? How does this influence the way we view sexual temptation?

+Given the Bible's portrayal of the human heart, why should we be hesitant to trust it when deciding what to do with our bodies?

+ Why do we need Christ to give us a new heart? How can this provide hope in the fight against sexual temptation?

Develop and post a personal tweet or Facebook status related to this session using the hashtag **#trueloveproject**

## 5) Purity From Within  (APPROXIMATELY 15 MINUTES)

Once group discussion has ended, watch the DVD segment *Purity From Within*. Instruct students to turn to page 38 in their student books to follow along. After the session, help students complete their video guides if they missed any points.

After the video, encourage students to complete both the Video Feedback and Reflect sections in Session 5 of the student book before the next time you meet. Explain that these sections will be used in group discussion during the next session. Close your time together in prayer.

## Leader Notes

From Clayton's teaching and your personal reflection, what are some highlights you intend to discuss during group time?

**5**

# session 5:
# PURITY
# FROM WITHIN

Yahweh, if You considered sins,
Lord, who could stand?
But with You there is forgiveness,
so that You may be revered.

**PSALM 130:3-4**

1) Session Introduction
2) Video Recap
3) Session Interview 📀 DVD
4) Group Discussion
5) Our Final Destination 📀 DVD

## 1) Session Introduction (APPROXIMATELY FIVE MINUTES)

Begin the fifth session by discussing the following questions:

+ What is the toughest test you've ever taken? Why was it so tough?
+ What's the most difficult project you've ever attempted? What made it difficult?
+ What are the hardest words you've ever had to say? What made them so hard to say?

We've all faced difficult things in our lives, but perhaps one of the most difficult things we've had to do is seek forgiveness or give forgiveness. Discuss why forgiveness is such a difficult thing, and why it is so vital when it somes to our sexuality.

## 2) Video Recap (APPROXIMATELY FIVE MINUTES)

To transition to the session interview, recap Clayton's teaching session by reminding students what it means for us, as sexual sinners, to be forgiven by a loving Father in heaven. Remind them what the Bible says about the topic of forgiveness—both receiving it and extending it to others—and what this means for those who have compromised their purity in the past. Finally, remind them that whether or not they have retained their physical purity, chances are they have failed at remaining pure within their heart. As such, they need to receive forgiveness and allow Jesus to purify their hearts from within.

### Main Thought:

Dealing with sexual sin involves receiving God's forgiveness, as well as extending forgiveness to others.

## 3) Session Interview 💿 (APPROXIMATELY 10 MINUTES)

After the recap/summary, play the session interview with Marian Jordan Ellis. Direct students to the group discussion page in their student books (p. 44). Point out the space provided for notes on the interview. Record some of your personal reflections below to discuss during Group Discussion.

## 4) Group Discussion (APPROXIMATELY 25 MINUTES)

✦ Briefly discuss highlights from the interview.

✦ Review the Video Guide and Video Feedback from Session 5 in the leader guide (pp. 36-37).

✦ Use the following questions to enhance your discussion.

> • What have you learned about God's forgiveness from this session?
>
> • How does knowing that our purity comes from Jesus help us in our fight for sexual purity? Why is it important to emphasize this point when we fall into sexual sin?
>
> • How does knowing our true identity in Christ influence us positively when making decisions about our purity?

✦ Direct students to complete the Highlights section of the Group Discussion page in their student books (p. 44). Allow time to answer and discuss these as a group.

✦ **ASK:** What actions do you need to take in response to what you've learned? Encourage students to list answers under Action Points. Below is a sample to prompt students.

### Action Points

✦ Confess and repent of the following sexual sin(s):
✦
✦

# Session 5: PURITY FROM WITHIN

Many people misunderstand the biblical view of sex and have experienced sexual sin as a result of sinfulness. That being said, it is important to emphasize our need to be forgiven and to forgive. Even if you have compromised on your physical or heart purity in the past, you are never beyond the grace of God's forgiveness. Through Christ, not only can forgiveness be received and extended, but purity can also be restored.

## video guide:

When it comes to the topic of forgiveness—from sexual sins or other sins—there are two realities you need to consider:

You may need to _receive_ God's forgiveness for the mistakes you've made.
You may need to _forgive_ someone for the sins they committed against you.

### RECEIVE GOD'S FORGIVENESS:

The first step to this kind of new beginning is to _confess_ your sin and _repent_ of your sin.

**CONFESS:** When we confess our sin to God, we are "_fessing_ up, admitting to, and agreeing with" God that we are _imperfect_ and sinful.

**REPENT:** To repent simply means to "turn _away_ and turn around."

### EXTEND FORGIVENESS TO OTHERS:

Forgiveness is how God _healed_ us.
Forgiveness is how we _heal_ ourselves.

# video feedback:

+ By realizing that sexual sin can be both physical (sexual activity before marriage, etc.) and of the heart (lust, coveting, etc.), why is it necessary to emphasize our need for forgiveness?

+ In light of the Bible's teaching that we should forgive in the same manner in which we have been forgiven, how should you respond toward those who have sinned against you?

+ Why is it important to emphasize both confession and repentance when it comes to dealing with past sexual sins? What does this look like practically?

+ If you have compromised in your path towards purity, how encouraging is it to hear that Christ is able to make you pure by His grace in your life? Explain.

Develop and post a personal tweet or Facebook status related to this session using the hashtag **#trueloveproject**

## 5) Our Final Destination  (APPROXIMATELY 15 MINUTES)

Once group discussion has ended, watch the DVD segment *Our Final Destination*. Instruct students to turn to page 46 in their student books to follow along. After the session, help students complete their video guides in case they missed a point.

After the video, encourage students to complete both the Video Feedback and Reflect sections in Session 6 of the student book before the next time you meet. Explain that these sections will be used in group discussion during the next session. Close your time together in prayer.

## Leader Notes

From Clayton's teaching and your personal reflection, what are some highlights you intend to discuss during group time?

# session 6:
# OUR FINAL DESTINATION

"My purity is for His delight primarily. If I am still single at age 70, my heart will be full of joy over the relationship I have shared with my regal King, thankful that immorality never harmed the depth of intimacy we have shared. As my King Regent, He has every right to all of me — including the sexual me. I am His alone. He is the main thing, the only thing that matters ultimately. I am waiting for unimaginable closeness with Him forever. And I want nothing on earth that impinges on my delight in Him forever."

**-DR. RICHARD ROSS,
CO-FOUNDER OF *TRUE LOVE WAITS***

1) Session Introduction
2) Video Recap
3) Session Interview 💿 **DVD**
4) Group Discussion
5) Hate It, Starve It, Outsmart It

## 1) Session Introduction (APPROXIMATELY FIVE MINUTES)

Begin the session by asking students the follow question:

✛  If I want to go to (name a prominent place in your area), which direction would I go from here?

Direct the student who answers to stand and point in that direction. Ask the other students if he/she is correct. If not, allow someone else to point in the right direction. Repeat this activity a few more times, substituting different regional or national locations. Discuss the importance of correct direction in arriving at the correct destination.

## 2) Video Recap (APPROXIMATELY FIVE MINUTES)

To transition to the session interview, recap Clayton's teaching session by reminding students what the study has covered thus far. Explain to them that there has been a progression throughout. We began by exploring God's Story, Jesus' lordship, and the Bible's commands on sex and purity. We then looked at the reality that we are all sinners, and our problem resides within our hearts. After emphasizing that we are incapable of making a lasting heart change, we spent an entire session on forgiveness— God's forgiveness toward us and our forgiveness toward others.

The latest video session discussed ways to fight sexual temptation through the power of the gospel. We looked at how our destination—or end goal—will influence our directions along the way. We also saw that one of the main points throughout this session was the notion that merely being found a virgin on one's honeymoon night is not the ultimate goal for Christians. Rather, our ultimate goal is to be found faithful to Christ at His return. Once Jesus becomes our final destination, we will want to pursue purity out of our love for Him.

### Main Thought:

When it comes to sexual purity, you have to determine where you are going and how you get there.

## 3) Session Interview 💿 (APPROXIMATELY 10 MINUTES)

After the recap, play the session interview with Jeff Bethke. Direct students to the group discussion page in their student books (p. 52). Point out the space provided for notes on the interview. Record some of your personal reflections below to discuss during Group Discussion.

## 4) Group Discussion (APPROXIMATELY 25 MINUTES)

✝ Briefly discuss highlights from the interview.

✝ Review the Video Guide and Video Feedback from Session 6 in the leader guide (pp. 42-43).

✝ Use the following questions to enhance your discussion.

- How could the pursuit of virginity become an idol in your heart? Why is it important to emphasize the pursuit of Jesus through sexual purity?

- Why is it important that we fight against the fleeting pleasures of sin by emphasizing the infinite pleasures found in Christ?

- Why is it important to be surrounded by Christian community in your personal fight for purity? How can you help serve your Christian brothers and sisters in their journey?

✝ Direct students to complete the Highlights section of the Group Discussion page in their student books (p. 52). Allow time to answer and discuss these as a group.

✝ **ASK:** What actions do you need to take in response to what you have learned? Encourage students to list their answers under the Action Points. Below is a sample to prompt students.

### Action Points

✝ Reevaluate my goals for staying pure. Make sure they are first and foremost about making much of Jesus in my life.

✝

✝

# Session 6: OUR FINAL DESTINATION

After having spent five sessions laying the biblical groundwork for God's view concerning Himself, ourselves, sex, and purity, we now turn our attention to practical ways these beliefs work themselves out in everyday life. In this session, we will focus not only on the end goal of our sexual purity, but also the end goal for all of our lives—Jesus.

## video guide:

### WHERE YOU ARE GOING:

It's not your intention that gets you to your destination. It's taking action by heading in the right direction.

Before you can strike out in the right direction, you must decide where it is you want to go.

The end goal is not to be a virgin on your wedding day. The end goal is to be found faithful on judgment day.

Jesus is the destination.

### HOW YOU GET THERE:

+ SUBMISSION:

+ DIRECTION:

+ INSTRUCTION:

+ ACTION:

+ DESTINATION:

# video feedback:

+ How would you explain the relationship between destination and directions? How does the former determine the latter?

+ Though staying a virgin before marriage is important and something that should be fought for, why should Jesus, and not virginity, be our end goal?

+ What practical steps can you take to honor and glorify Jesus through your sexuality?

+ What stood out to you in this session? Why? How do these ideas cause you to reconsider your direction in your path toward purity?

Develop and post a personal tweet or Facebook status related to this session using the hashtag #trueloveproject

## 5) Hate It, Starve It, Outsmart It  (APPROXIMATELY 15 MINUTES)

Once group discussion has ended, watch the DVD segment *Hate It, Starve It, Outsmart It*. Instruct students to turn to page 54 in their student books to follow along. After the session, help students complete their video guides if they missed any points.

After the video, encourage students to complete both the Video Feedback and Reflect sections in Session 7 of the student book before the next time you meet. Explain that these sections will be used in group discussion during the next session. Close your time together in prayer.


## Leader Notes

From Clayton's teaching and your personal reflection, what are some highlights you intend to discuss during group time?

**7**

in
the
as a
sation
g was

ket to
, and

would

# session 7:
# HATE IT, STARVE IT, OUTSMART IT

You will never win the battle with sin by just trying harder. Effort alone is not enough. Sin is stronger and more experienced than you, and like a serial killer it will not settle for anything other than the complete taking of your life. If you want to defeat sin and temptation, you have to have a better plan, one capable of a multi-faceted attack.

**—CLAYTON KING**

1) Session Introduction
2) Video Recap
3) Session Interview 📀 DVD
4) Group Discussion
5) Sex, God's Glory, and Your Mission 📀 DVD

## 1) Session Introduction (APPROXIMATELY FIVE MINUTES)

Begin the session by grouping students into small teams. Provide each team with construction paper, popsicle sticks, and paper clips. Inform teams that the challenge is to build the tallest tower using only the supplies given withing the next five minutes. Start the timer and allow teams to work. After five minutes, call time and judge which team is the winner. Give prizes to the winning team. Ask:

✝ How many of you took the time to make a plan before you started working? Did it make a difference? Why or why not?

Point out that when it comes to maintaing sexual purity, having a battle plan is essential to success.

## 2) Video Recap (APPROXIMATELY FIVE MINUTES)

To transition to the session interview, recap Clayton's teaching session by reminding students of the main thought in *Hate It, Starve It, Outsmart It*. Remind them of the importance of developing a personal strategy to adopt and adapt in their fight for purity. This is extremely important because it is difficult to glorify God through our sexuality apart from having a plan of action. Summarize the biblical plan of action that was discussed in Psalm 119, where the psalmist fights sin through hating it, starving it, and outsmarting it.

## Main Thought:

Fighting sexual sin and temptation will require you to hate it, starve it, and outsmart it.

# 3) Session Interview 📀 (APPROXIMATELY 10 MINUTES)

After the recap/summary, play the session interview with Steven and Holly Furtick. Direct students to the group discussion page in their student books (p. 60). Point out the space provided for notes on the interview. Record some of your personal reflections below to discuss during Group Discussion.

# 4) Group Discussion (APPROXIMATELY 25 MINUTES)

+ Briefly discuss highlights from the interview.

+ Review the Video Guide and Video Feedback from Session 7 in the leader guide (pp. 48-49).

+ Use the following questions to enhance your discussion.

> • What have you learned about your own battle plan when it comes to pursuing sexual purity?
>
> • How do daily habits influence our decisions regarding sex and purity?
>
> • Why is it important to implement new habits in your daily life? How can this be done?

+ Direct students to complete the Highlights section of the Group Discussion page in their student books (p. 60). Allow time to answer and discuss these as a group.

+ **ASK:** What actions do you need to take in response to what you have learned? Encourage students to list their answers under the Action Points. Below is a sample to prompt students.

## Action Points

+ I'm going to starve and outsmart my sexual struggles by adopting the following daily strategies:

+

+

# Session 7: HATE IT, STARVE IT, OUTSMART IT

Once we have decided on our final arriving point—Jesus—and have moved in the direction of pursuing Him, it is important for us to develop and maintain a plan of action to help us reach our goal. This plan of action is not an attempt to create artificial rules or standards that we live by in order to feel self-righteous. Instead, it is a biblical response to the grace of God working through our lives. In this session, we are going to explore some proactive ways to fight sexual temptation and cultivate genuine desire for purity and holiness.

## video guide:

We are to be pro-active when it comes to _fighting_ remaining sin in our lives, and one of the ways to do so is to have a biblical plan of attack.

### HATE IT:

### STARVE IT:

### OUTSMART IT:

You will need to _adopt_ this battle plan and _adapt_ it to your certain situation.

You are not fighting _for_ victory; you are fighting _from_ victory.

# video feedback:

+ Why is it important to have a biblical plan of action when it comes to fighting against sin in your life?

+ What do you think about the psalmist's battle plan? How could you adopt and adapt it to your personal struggles?

+ Explain why having a plan isn't an attempt to earn grace but rather a natural response to grace.

+ What additional things can you do to help guard you on the path toward Christ?

Develop and post a personal tweet or Facebook status related to this session using the hashtag **#trueloveproject**

## 5) Sex, God's Glory, and Your Mission  (APPROXIMATELY 15 MINUTES)

Once group discussion has ended, watch the DVD segment *Sex, God's Glory, and Your Mission*. Instruct students to turn to page 62 in their student books to follow along. After the session, help students complete their video guides if they missed any points.

After the video, encourage students to complete both the Video Feedback and Reflect sections in Session 8 of the student book before the next time you meet. Explain that these sections will be used in group discussion during the next session. Close your time together in prayer.

## Leader Notes

From Clayton's teaching and your personal reflection, what are some highlights you intend to discuss during group time?

**8**

# session 8:
# SEX, GOD'S GLORY, AND YOUR MISSION

When Jesus is Lord of your life, He is Lord of all of your life, including your physical and emotional desires for romance, love, and sex. When you are committed to living a holy life that is set apart for Him, you live a life of worship to Christ and a life of witness to the world.

1) Session Introduction
2) Video Recap
3) Session Interview 💿 DVD
4) Group Discussion
5) Closing Remarks 💿 DVD

## 1) Session Introduction (APPROXIMATELY FIVE MINUTES)

Begin the session by asking the following questions:

✝ How many of you are involved in a school sports team or an extracurricular activity where you represent your school (such as band, drama, chorus, etc.)? How do your actions on and off the "field" reflect on your school?

Remind students that whenever we put on a school uniform or perform under the name of that school, our performance, words, and actions reflect the school we represent. In the same way, if we claim to be Christ-followers, then our decisions and actions reflect on Him and His name, especially in the area of our sexuality. Emphasize that we are witnesses of the gospel and on mission for Christ in everything we do.

## 2) Video Recap (APPROXIMATELY FIVE MINUTES)

To transition to the session interview, recap what was discussed on the *Sex, God's Glory, and Your Mission* video. Remind students of the connection between one's beliefs about sex and purity and that person's worship and witness in the world. Also recall that sexual decisions are not segregated from other parts of your Christian life. What you do with your heart, mind, and body, as well as how you respect the bodies of others, is a witness to those around you. When it comes down to it, we either make much of Christ by fighting for purity, or we show Him to be irrelevant to us by pursuing sexual sin.

### Main Thought:
Our beliefs and actions regarding sexual purity says something about God's glory and our witness to the world.

## 3) Session Interview 📀 (APPROXIMATELY 10 MINUTES)

After the recap/summary, play the session interview with Derwin and Vicky Gray. Direct students to the group discussion page in their student books (p. 68). Point out the space provided for notes on the interview. Record some of your personal reflections below to discuss during Group Discussion.

## 4) Group Discussion (APPROXIMATELY 25 MINUTES)

+ Briefly discuss highlights from the interview.

+ Review the Video Guide and Video Feedback from Session 8 in the leader guide (pp. 54-55).

+ Use the following questions to enhance your discussion.

- • What is the connection between the way we treat our bodies and God's glory?

- • What is the connection between the way we treat our bodies and our witness for Christ?

- • How has this study on sex and purity impacted your life? How will you treat others differently as a result?

+ Direct students to complete the Highlights section of the Group Discussion page in their student books (p. 68). Allow time to answer and discuss these as a group.

+ **ASK:** What actions do you need to take in response to what you have learned? Encourage students to list their answers under the Action Points. Below is a sample to prompt students.

### Action Points

+ Be more vocal about my Christian beliefs regarding sex and purity to those around me.

+

+

# Session 8: SEX, GOD'S GLORY, AND YOUR MISSION

Our actions communicate what we really believe to both ourselves and others. In the case of sexuality, it is easy to see that what we do with our bodies actually communicates whether we agree with God on the subject or not. Those actions also communicate a positive witness of the gospel to those who are watching. In the end, we need to realize that sex and purity aren't just about sex and purity—they are ultimately about God, His Glory, and our mission here on earth.

## video guide:

God didn't save you so you could _sit_. He saved you so you could serve.

He didn't save you to wait around. He saved you to work and _worship_.

Our worship is our _witness_ to the world.

It is an act of worship to stand against the tide of _sexual sin_ and temptation and to declare, "Jesus is Lord and I belong to Him. I will do what He says."

I'm not promising you that people will _celebrate_ your commitment to purity or applaud your battle for holiness.

You represent the _kingdom_ of God and you carry the gospel of Jesus Christ with you everywhere you go.

So remember, the _gospel_ impacts your purity, and your purity says something to the world about your commitment to the _gospel_.

# video feedback

+ Summarize Clayton's connection between sex, worship, and witness. Why is it important to think of this topic in such a way?

+ How has Clayton's personal story of standing up and speaking encouraged you to do the same?

+ If you haven't been the greatest witness for Christ in this area of your life, how has this study encouraged you to change?

+ How has this study encouraged you to live for Christ in the area of your sexuality? What will you do differently from this point forward?

Develop and post a personal tweet or Facebook status related to this session using the hashtag **#trueloveproject**

# 5) Closing Remarks 💿 (APPROXIMATELY 15 MINUTES)

Once group discussion has ended, watch the DVD segment *Closing Remarks*.

## True Love Waits Commitment

The final video segment marks the end of our study. The length of the final video allows you to wrap things up in a manner of your own choosing. For example, you can give students an opportunity to respond to what they have heard over these last several weeks. As a way for students to display the internal commitment to Christ in the pursuit of purity they have made, consider using the *True Love Waits* commitment cards. A commitment card is found in the back of every student book. You may also plan beforehand to have a few students share what this study has meant to them, or perhaps consider closing with a personal challenge that encourages students to live in light of what they have learned throughout the study. Whatever route you choose, be sure to emphasize once more the heart of the study—how the gospel of Jesus Christ defines their personal purity.

By the time you have reached this section, you have hopefully gone through all eight sessions of the *True Love Project*. It is our hope and prayer that by this point, the words on this commitment card are an accurate reflection of where your heart is right now in regards to your commitment to Christ in the pursuit of purity. We hope that by this time you have realized that the battle for purity is a lifelong commitment, fought in the grace and strength that God supplies. However, it also a battle that has already been won on our behalf since it is the gospel that defines our purity. By signing this card, you are externally confirming this internal commitment.

## True Love Waits Commitment

In light of who God is, what Christ has done for me, and who I am in Him, from this day forward I commit myself to Him in the lifelong pursuit of purity. By His grace, I will continually present myself to Him as a living sacrifice, holy and pleasing to God.

SIGNATURE _____

DATE _____

**true
love
waits.**